Beasley's Christmas Party

By
Booth Tarkington

I

The maple-bordered street was as still as a country Sunday; so quiet that there seemed an echo to my footsteps. It was four o'clock in the morning; clear October moonlight misted through the thinning foliage to the shadowy sidewalk and lay like a transparent silver fog upon the house of my admiration, as I strode along, returning from my first night's work on the "Wainwright Morning Despatch."

I had already marked that house as the finest (to my taste) in Wainwright, though hitherto, on my excursions to this metropolis, the state capital, I was not without a certain native jealousy that Spencerville, the county-seat where I lived, had nothing so good. Now, however, I approached its purlieus with a pleasure in it quite unalloyed, for I was at last myself a resident (albeit of only one day's standing) of Wainwright, and the house—though I had not even an idea who lived there—part of my possessions as a citizen. Moreover, I might enjoy the warmer pride of a next-door-neighbor, for Mrs. Apperthwaite's, where I had taken a room, was just beyond.

This was the quietest part of Wainwright; business stopped short of it, and the "fashionable residence section" had overleaped this "forgotten backwater," leaving it undisturbed and unchanging, with that look about it which is the quality of few urban quarters, and eventually of none, as a town grows to be a city—the look of still being a neighborhood. This friendliness of appearance was largely the emanation of the homely and beautiful house which so greatly pleased my fancy.

It might be difficult to say why I thought it the "finest" house in Wainwright, for a simpler structure would be hard to imagine; it was merely a big, old-fashioned brick house, painted brown and very plain, set well away from the street among some splendid forest trees, with a fair spread of flat lawn. But it gave back a great deal for your glance, just as some people do. It was a large house, as I say, yet it looked not like a mansion but like a home; and made you wish that you lived in it. Or, driving by, of an evening, you would have liked to hitch your horse and go in; it spoke so surely of hearty, old-fashioned people living there, who would welcome you merrily.

It looked like a house where there were a grandfather and a

grandmother; where holidays were warmly kept; where there were boisterous family reunions to which uncles and aunts, who had been born there, would return from no matter what distances; a house where big turkeys would be on the table often; where one called "the hired man" (and named either Abner or Ole) would crack walnuts upon a flat-iron clutched between his knees on the back porch; it looked like a house where they played charades; where there would be long streamers of evergreen and dozens of wreaths of holly at Christmas-time; where there were tearful, happy weddings and great throwings of rice after little brides, from the broad front steps: in a word, it was the sort of a house to make the hearts of spinsters and bachelors very lonely and wistful—and that is about as near as I can come to my reason for thinking it the finest house in Wainwright.

The moon hung kindly above its level roof in the silence of that October morning, as I checked my gait to loiter along the picket fence; but suddenly the house showed a light of its own. The spurt of a match took my eye to one of the upper windows, then a steadier glow of orange told me that a lamp was lighted. The window was opened, and a man looked out and whistled loudly.

I stopped, thinking that he meant to attract my attention; that something might be wrong; that perhaps some one was needed to go for a doctor. My mistake was immediately evident, however; I stood in the shadow of the trees bordering the sidewalk, and the man at the window had not seen me.

"Boy! Boy!" he called, softly. "Where are you, Simpledoria?"

He leaned from the window, looking downward. "Why, THERE you are!" he exclaimed, and turned to address some invisible person within the room. "He's right there, underneath the window. I'll bring him up." He leaned out again. "Wait there, Simpledoria!" he called. "I'll be down in a jiffy and let you in."

Puzzled, I stared at the vacant lawn before me. The clear moonlight revealed it brightly, and it was empty of any living presence; there were no bushes nor shrubberies—nor even shadows—that could have been mistaken for a boy, if "Simpledoria" WAS a boy. There was no dog in sight; there was no cat; there was nothing beneath the window except thick, close-cropped grass.

A light shone in the hallway behind the broad front doors; one of these was opened, and revealed in silhouette the tall, thin figure of a man in a long, old-fashioned dressing-gown.

"Simpledoria," he said, addressing the night air with considerable severity, "I don't know what to make of you. You might have caught your death of cold, roving out at such an hour. But there," he continued, more indulgently; "wipe your feet on the mat and come in. You're safe NOW!"

He closed the door, and I heard him call to some one up-stairs, as he rearranged the fastenings:

"Simpledoria is all right—only a little chilled. I'll bring him up to your fire."

I went on my way in a condition of astonishment that engendered, almost, a doubt of my eyes; for if my sight was unimpaired and myself not subject to optical or mental delusion, neither boy nor dog nor bird nor cat, nor any other object of this visible world, had entered that opened door. Was my "finest" house, then, a place of call for wandering ghosts, who came home to roost at four in the morning?

It was only a step to Mrs. Apperthwaite's; I let myself in with the key that good lady had given me, stole up to my room, went to my window, and stared across the yard at the house next door. The front window in the second story, I decided, necessarily belonged to that room in which the lamp had been lighted; but all was dark there now. I went to bed, and dreamed that I was out at sea in a fog, having embarked on a transparent vessel whose preposterous name, inscribed upon glass life-belts, depending here and there from an invisible rail, was SIMPLEDORIA.

II

Mrs. Apperthwaite's was a commodious old house, the greater part of it of about the same age, I judged, as its neighbor; but the late Mr. Apperthwaite had caught the Mansard fever of the late 'Seventies, and the building-disease, once fastened upon him, had never known a convalescence, but, rather, a series of relapses, the tokens of which, in the nature of a cupola and a couple of frame turrets, were terrifyingly apparent. These romantic misplacements seemed to me not inharmonious with the library, a cheerful and pleasantly shabby apartment down-stairs, where I found (over a substratum of history, encyclopaedia, and family Bible) some worn old volumes of Godey's Lady's Book, an early edition of Cooper's works; Scott, Bulwer, Macaulay, Byron, and Tennyson, complete; some odd volumes of Victor Hugo, of the elder Dumas, of Flaubert, of Gautier, and of Balzac; Clarissa, Lalla Rookh, The Alhambra, Beulah, Uarda, Lucile, Uncle Tom's Cabin, Ben-Hur, Trilby, She, Little Lord Fauntleroy; and of a later decade, there were novels about those delicately tangled emotions experienced by the supreme few; and stories of adventurous royalty; tales of "clean-limbed young American manhood;" and some thin volumes of rather precious verse.

'Twas amid these romantic scenes that I awaited the sound of the lunch-bell (which for me was the announcement of breakfast), when I arose from my first night's slumbers under Mrs. Apperthwaite's roof; and I wondered if the books were a fair mirror of Miss Apperthwaite's mind (I had been told that Mrs. Apperthwaite had a daughter). Mrs. Apperthwaite herself, in her youth, might have sat to an illustrator of Scott or Bulwer. Even now you could see she had come as near being romantically beautiful as was consistently proper for such a timid, gentle little gentlewoman as she was. Reduced, by her husband's insolvency (coincident with his demise) to "keeping boarders," she did it gracefully, as if the urgency thereto were only a spirit of quiet hospitality. It should be added in haste that she set an excellent table.

Moreover, the guests who gathered at her board were of a very attractive description, as I decided the instant my eye fell upon the lady who sat opposite me at lunch. I knew at once that she was Miss Apperthwaite, she "went so," as they say, with her mother; nothing could have been more suitable. Mrs. Apperthwaite was the kind of woman whom you would expect to have a beautiful daughter, and Miss Apperthwaite more than fulfilled her mother's promise.

I guessed her to be more than Juliet Capulet's age, indeed, yet still between that and the perfect age of woman. She was of a larger, fuller, more striking type than Mrs. Apperthwaite, a bolder type, one might put it—though she might have been a great deal bolder than Mrs. Apperthwaite without being bold. Certainly she was handsome enough to make it difficult for a young fellow to keep from staring at her. She had an abundance of very soft, dark hair, worn almost severely, as if its profusion necessitated repression; and I am compelled to admit that her fine eyes expressed a distant contemplation—obviously of habit not of mood—so pronounced that one of her enemies (if she had any) might have described them as "dreamy."

Only one other of my own sex was present at the lunch-table, a Mr. Dowden, an elderly lawyer and politician of whom I had heard, and to whom Mrs. Apperthwaite, coming in after the rest of us were seated, introduced me. She made the presentation general; and I had the experience of receiving a nod and a slow glance, in which there was a sort of dusky, estimating brilliance, from the beautiful lady opposite me.

It might have been better mannered for me to address myself to Mr. Dowden, or one of the very nice elderly women, who were my fellow-guests, than to open a conversation with Miss Apperthwaite; but I did not stop to think of that.

"You have a splendid old house next door to you here, Miss Apperthwaite," I said. "It's a privilege to find it in view from my window."

There was a faint stir as of some consternation in the little company. The elderly ladies stopped talking abruptly and exchanged glances, though this was not of my observation at the moment, I think, but recurred to my consciousness later, when I had perceived my blunder.

"May I ask who lives there?" I pursued.

Miss Apperthwaite allowed her noticeable lashes to cover her eyes for an instant, then looked up again.

"A Mr. Beasley," she said.

"Not the Honorable David Beasley!" I exclaimed.

"Yes," she returned, with a certain gravity which I afterward wished had checked me. "Do you know him?"

"Not in person," I explained. "You see, I've written a good deal about him. I was with the "Spencerville Journal" until a few days ago, and even in the country we know who's who in politics over the state. Beasley's the man that went to Congress and never made a speech—never made even a motion to adjourn—but got everything his district wanted. There's talk of him now for Governor."

"Indeed?"

"And so it's the Honorable David Beasley who lives in that splendid place. How curious that is!"

"Why?" asked Miss Apperthwaite.

"It seems too big for one man," I answered; "and I've always had the impression Mr. Beasley was a bachelor."

"Yes," she said, rather slowly, "he is."

"But of course he doesn't live there all alone," I supposed, aloud, "probably he has—"

"No. There's no one else—except a couple of colored servants."

"What a crime!" I exclaimed. "If there ever was a house meant for a large family, that one is. Can't you almost hear it crying out for heaps and heaps of romping children? I should think—"

I was interrupted by a loud cough from Mr. Dowden, so abrupt and artificial that his intention to check the flow of my innocent prattle was embarrassingly obvious—even to me!

"Can you tell me," he said, leaning forward and following up the interruption as hastily as possible, "what the farmers were getting for their wheat when you left Spencerville?"

"Ninety-four cents," I answered, and felt my ears growing red with mortification. Too late, I remembered that the new-comer in a community should guard his tongue among the natives until he has unravelled the skein of their relationships, alliances, feuds, and private wars—a precept not unlike the classic injunction:

"Yes, my darling daughter.
Hang your clothes on a hickory limb,
But don't go near the water."

However, in my confusion I warmly regretted my failure to follow it, and resolved not to blunder again.

Mr. Dowden thanked me for the information for which he had no real desire, and, the elderly ladies again taking up (with all too evident relief) their various mild debates, he inquired if I played bridge. "But I forget," he added. "Of course you'll be at the 'Despatch' office in the evenings, and can't be here." After which he immediately began to question me about my work, making his determination to give me no opportunity again to mention the Honorable David Beasley unnecessarily conspicuous, as I thought.

I could only conclude that some unpleasantness had arisen between himself and Beasley, probably of political origin, since they were both in politics, and of personal (and consequently bitter) development; and that Mr. Dowden found the mention of Beasley not only unpleasant to himself but a possible embarrassment to the ladies (who, I supposed, were aware of the quarrel) on his account.

After lunch, not having to report at the office immediately, I took unto myself the solace of a cigar, which kept me company during a stroll about Mrs. Apperthwaite's capacious yard. In the rear I found an old-fashioned rose-garden—the bushes long since bloomless and now brown with autumn —and I paced its gravelled paths up and down, at the same time favoring Mr. Beasley's house with a covert study that would have done credit to a porch-climber, for the sting of my blunder at the table was quiescent, or at least neutralized, under the itch of a curiosity far from satisfied concerning the interesting premises next door. The gentleman in the dressing-gown, I was sure, could have been no other than the Honorable David Beasley himself. He came not in eyeshot now, neither he nor any other; there was no sign of life about the place. That portion of his yard which lay behind the house was not within my vision, it is true, his property being here separated from Mrs. Apperthwaite's by a board fence higher than a tall man could reach; but there was no sound from the other side of this partition, save that caused by the quiet movement of rusty leaves in the breeze.

My cigar was at half-length when the green lattice door of Mrs. Apperthwaite's back porch was opened and Miss Apperthwaite, bearing a saucer of milk, issued therefrom, followed, hastily, by a very white, fat cat, with a pink ribbon round its neck, a vibrant nose, and fixed, voracious eyes uplifted to the saucer. The lady and her cat offered to view a group as pretty as a popular painting; it was even improved when, stooping, Miss Apperthwaite set the saucer upon the ground, and, continuing in that posture, stroked the cat. To bend so far is a test of a woman's grace, I have observed.

She turned her face toward me and smiled. "I'm almost at the age, you see."

"What age?" I asked, stupidly enough.

"When we take to cats," she said, rising. "Spinsterhood' we like to call it. 'Single-blessedness!'"

"That is your kind heart. You decline to make one of us happy to the despair of all the rest."

She laughed at this, though with no very genuine mirth, I marked, and let my 1830 attempt at gallantry pass without other retort.

"You seemed interested in the old place yonder." She indicated Mr. Beasley's house with a nod.

"Oh, I understood my blunder," I said, quickly. "I wish I had known the subject was embarrassing or unpleasant to Mr. Dowden."

"What made you think that?"

"Surely," I said, "you saw how pointedly he cut me off."

"Yes," she returned, thoughtfully. "He rather did; it's true. At least, I see how you got that impression." She seemed to muse upon this, letting her eyes fall; then, raising them, allowed her far-away gaze to rest upon the house beyond the fence, and said, "It IS an interesting old place."

"And Mr. Beasley himself—" I began.

"Oh," she said, "HE isn't interesting. That's his trouble!"

"You mean his trouble not to—"

She interrupted me, speaking with sudden, surprising energy, "I mean he's a man of no imagination."

"No imagination!" I exclaimed.

"None in the world! Not one ounce of imagination! Not one grain!"

"Then who," I cried—"or what—is Simpledoria?"

"Simple—what?" she said, plainly mystified.

"Simpledoria."

"Simpledoria?" she repeated, and laughed. "What in the world is that?"

"You never heard of it before?"

"Never in my life."

"You've lived next door to Mr. Beasley a long time, haven't you?"

"All my life."

"And I suppose you must know him pretty well."

"What next?" she said, smiling.

"You said he lived there all alone," I went on, tentatively.

"Except for an old colored couple, his servants."

"Can you tell me—" I hesitated. "Has he ever been thought—well, 'queer'?"

"Never!" she answered, emphatically. "Never anything so exciting! Merely deadly and hopelessly commonplace." She picked up the saucer, now exceedingly empty, and set it upon a shelf by the lattice door. "What was it about—what was that name?—'Simpledoria'?"

"I will tell you," I said. And I related in detail the singular performance of which I had been a witness in the late moonlight before that morning's dawn. As I talked, we half unconsciously moved across the lawn together, finally seating ourselves upon a bench beyond the rose-beds and near the high fence. The interest my companion exhibited in the narration might have surprised me had my nocturnal experience itself been less surprising. She interrupted me now and then with little, half-checked ejaculations of acute wonder, but sat for the most part with her elbow on her knee and her chin in her hand, her face turned eagerly to mine and her lips parted in half-breathless attention. There was nothing "far away" about her eyes now; they were widely and intently alert.

When I finished, she shook her head slowly, as if quite dumfounded, and altered her position, leaning against the back of the bench and gazing straight before her without speaking. It was plain that her neighbor's extraordinary behavior had revealed a phase of his character novel enough to be startling.

"One explanation might be just barely possible," I said. "If it is, it is the most remarkable case of somnambulism on record. Did you ever hear of Mr. Beasley's walking in his—"

She touched me lightly but peremptorily on the arm in warning, and I stopped. On the other side of the board fence a door opened creakily, and there sounded a loud and cheerful voice—that of the gentleman in the dressing-gown.

"HERE we come!" it said; "me and big Bill Hammersley. I want to show Bill I can jump ANYWAYS three times as far as he can! Come on, Bill."

"Is that Mr. Beasley's voice?" I asked, under my breath.

Miss Apperthwaite nodded in affirmation.

"Could he have heard me?"

"No," she whispered. "He's just come out of the house." And then to herself, "Who under heaven is Bill Hammersley? I never heard of HIM!"

"Of course, Bill," said the voice beyond the fence, "if you're afraid I'll beat you TOO badly, you've still got time to back out. I did understand you to kind of hint that you were considerable of a jumper, but if—What? What'd you say, Bill?" There ensued a moment's complete silence. "Oh, all right," the voice then continued. "You say you're in this to win, do you? Well, so'm I, Bill Hammersley; so'm I. Who'll go first? Me? All right—from the edge of the walk here. Now then! One—two—three! HA!"

A sound came to our ears of some one landing heavily—and at full length, it seemed—on the turf, followed by a slight, rusty groan in the same voice. "Ugh! Don't you laugh, Bill Hammersley! I haven't jumped as much as I OUGHT to, these last twenty years; I reckon I've kind of lost the hang of it. Aha!" There were indications that Mr. Beasley was picking himself up, and brushing his trousers with his hands. "Now, it's your turn, Bill. What say?" Silence again, followed by, "Yes, I'll make Simpledoria get out of the way. Come here, Simpledoria. Now, Bill, put your heels together on the edge of the walk. That's right. All ready? Now then! One for the money —two for the show—three to make ready—and four for to GO!" Another silence. "By jingo, Bill Hammersley, you've beat me! Ha, ha! That WAS a jump! What say?" Silence once more. "You say you can do even better than that? Now, Bill, don't brag. Oh! you say you've often jumped farther? Oh! you say that was up in Scotland, where you had a spring-board? Oho! All right; let's see how far you can jump when you really try. There! Heels on the walk again. That's right; swing your arms. One—two—three! THERE you go!" Another silence. "ZING! Well, sir, I'll be e-tarnally snitched to flinders if you didn't do it THAT time, Bill Hammersley! I see I never really saw any jumping before in all my born days. It's eleven feet if it's an inch. What? You say you—"

I heard no more, for Miss Apperthwaite, her face flushed and her eyes shining, beckoned me imperiously to follow her, and departed so hurriedly that it might be said she ran.

"I don't know," said I, keeping at her elbow, "whether it's more like Alice or the interlocutor's conversation at a minstrel show."

"Hush!" she warned me, though we were already at a safe distance, and did not speak again until we had reached the front walk. There she paused, and I noted that she was trembling—and, no doubt correctly, judged her emotion to be that of consternation.

"There was no one THERE!" she exclaimed. "He was all by himself! It was just the same as what you saw last night!"

"Evidently."

"Did it sound to you"—there was a little awed tremor in her voice that I found very appealing—"did it sound to you like a person who'd lost his MIND?"

"I don't know," I said. "I don't know at all what to make of it."

"He couldn't have been"—her eyes grew very wide—"intoxicated!"

"No. I'm sure it wasn't that."

"Then *I* don't know what to make of it, either. All that wild talk about 'Bill Hammersley' and 'Simpledoria' and spring-boards in Scotland and—"

"And an eleven-foot jump," I suggested.

"Why, there's no more a 'Bill Hammersley,'" she cried, with a gesture of excited emphasis, "than there is a 'Simpledoria'!"

"So it appears," I agreed.

"He's lived there all alone," she said, solemnly, "in that big house, so long, just sitting there evening after evening all by himself, never going out, never reading anything, not even thinking; but just sitting and sitting and sitting and SITTING—Well," she broke off, suddenly, shook the frown from her forehead, and made me the offer of a dazzling smile, "there's no use bothering one's own head about it."

"I'm glad to have a fellow-witness," I said. "It's so eerie I might have concluded there was something the matter with ME."

"You're going to your work?" she asked, as I turned toward the gate. "I'm very glad I don't have to go to mine."

"Yours?" I inquired, rather blankly.

"I teach algebra and plain geometry at the High School," said this surprising young woman. "Thank Heaven, it's Saturday! I'm reading Les Miserables for the seventh time, and I'm going to have a real ORGY over Gervaise and the barricade this afternoon!"

III

I do not know why it should have astonished me to find that Miss Apperthwaite was a teacher of mathematics except that (to my inexperienced eye) she didn't look it. She looked more like Charlotte Corday!

I had the pleasure of seeing her opposite me at lunch the next day (when Mr. Dowden kept me occupied with Spencerville politics, obviously from fear that I would break out again), but no stroll in the yard with her rewarded me afterward, as I dimly hoped, for she disappeared before I left the table, and I did not see her again for a fortnight. On week-days she did not return to the house for lunch, my only meal at Mrs. Apperthwaite's (I dined at a restaurant near the "Despatch" office), and she was out of town for a little visit, her mother informed us, over the following Saturday and Sunday. She was not altogether out of my thoughts, however—indeed, she almost divided them with the Honorable David Beasley.

A better view which I was afforded of this gentleman did not lessen my interest in him; increased it rather; it also served to make the extraordinary didoes of which he had been the virtuoso and I the audience more than ever profoundly inexplicable. My glimpse of him in the lighted doorway had given me the vaguest impression of his appearance, but one afternoon—a few days after my interview with Miss Apperthwaite—I was starting for the office and met him full-face-on as he was turning in at his gate. I took as careful invoice of him as I could without conspicuously glaring.

There was something remarkably "taking," as we say, about this man— something easy and genial and quizzical and careless. He was the kind of person you LIKE to meet on the street; whose cheerful passing sends you on feeling indefinably a little gayer than you did. He was tall, thin—even gaunt, perhaps—and his face was long, rather pale, and shrewd and gentle; something in its oddity not unremindful of the late Sol Smith Russell. His hat was tilted back a little, the slightest bit to one side, and the sparse, brownish hair above his high forehead was going to be gray before long. He looked about forty.

The truth is, I had expected to see a cousin german to Don Quixote; I had thought to detect signs and gleams of wildness, however slight—

something a little "off." One glance of that kindly and humorous eye told me such expectation had been nonsense. Odd he might have been— Gadzooks! he looked it—but "queer"? Never. The fact that Miss Apperthwaite could picture such a man as this "sitting and sitting and sitting" himself into any form of mania or madness whatever spoke loudly of her own imagination, indeed! The key to "Simpledoria" was to be sought under some other mat.

... As I began to know some of my co-laborers on the "Despatch," and to pick up acquaintances, here and there, about town, I sometimes made Mr. Beasley the subject of inquiry. Everybody knew him. "Oh yes, I know Dave BEASLEY!" would come the reply, nearly always with a chuckling sort of laugh. I gathered that he had a name for "easy-going" which amounted to eccentricity. It was said that what the ward-heelers and camp-followers got out of him in campaign times made the political managers cry. He was the first and readiest prey for every fraud and swindler that came to Wainwright, I heard, and yet, in spite of this and of his hatred of "speech-making" ("He's as silent as Grant!" said one informant), he had a large practice, and was one of the most successful lawyers in the state.

One story they told of him (or, as they were more apt to put it, "on" him) was repeated so often that I saw it had become one of the town's traditions. One bitter evening in February, they related, he was approached upon the street by a ragged, whining, and shivering old reprobate, notorious for the various ingenuities by which he had worn out the patience of the charity organizations. He asked Beasley for a dime. Beasley had no money in his pockets, but gave the man his overcoat, went home without any himself, and spent six weeks in bed with a bad case of pneumonia as the direct result. His beneficiary sold the overcoat, and invested the proceeds in a five-day's spree, in the closing scenes of which a couple of brickbats were featured to high, spectacular effect. One he sent through a jeweller's show-window in an attempt to intimidate some wholly imaginary pursuers, the other he projected at a perfectly actual policeman who was endeavoring to soothe him. The victim of Beasley's charity and the officer were then borne to the hospital in company.

It was due in part to recollections of this legend and others of a similar character that people laughed when they said, "Oh yes, I know Dave BEASLEY!"

Altogether, I should say, Beasley was about the most popular man in

Wainwright. I could discover nowhere anything, however, to shed the faintest light upon the mystery of Bill Hammersley and Simpledoria. It was not until the Sunday of Miss Apperthwaite's absence that the revelation came.

That afternoon I went to call upon the widow of a second-cousin of mine; she lived in a cottage not far from Mrs. Apperthwaite's, upon the same street. I found her sitting on a pleasant veranda, with boxes of flowering plants along the railing, though Indian summer was now close upon departure. She was rocking meditatively, and held a finger in a morocco volume, apparently of verse, though I suspected she had been better entertained in the observation of the people and vehicles decorously passing along the sunlit thoroughfare within her view.

We exchanged inevitable questions and news of mutual relatives; I had told her how I liked my work and what I thought of Wainwright, and she was congratulating me upon having found so pleasant a place to live as Mrs. Apperthwaite's, when she interrupted herself to smile and nod a cordial greeting to two gentlemen driving by in a phaeton. They waved their hats to her gayly, then leaned back comfortably against the cushions—and if ever two men were obviously and incontestably on the best of terms with each other, THESE two were. They were David Beasley and Mr. Dowden. "I do wish," said my cousin, resuming her rocking—"I do wish dear David Beasley would get a new trap of some kind; that old phaeton of his is a disgrace! I suppose you haven't met him? Of course, living at Mrs. Apperthwaite's, you wouldn't be apt to."

"But what is he doing with Mr. Dowden?" I asked.

She lifted her eyebrows. "Why—taking him for a drive, I suppose."

"No. I mean—how do they happen to be together?"

"Why shouldn't they be? They're old friends—"

"They ARE!" And, in answer to her look of surprise, I explained that I had begun to speak of Beasley at Mrs. Apperthwaite's, and described the abruptness with which Dowden had changed the subject.

"I see," my cousin nodded, comprehendingly. "That's simple enough. George Dowden didn't want you to talk of Beasley THERE. I suppose it may have been a little embarrassing for everybody—especially if Ann Apperthwaite heard you."

"Ann? That's Miss Apperthwaite? Yes; I was speaking directly to her. Why SHOULDN'T she have heard me? She talked of him herself a little later—and at some length, too."

"She DID!" My cousin stopped rocking, and fixed me with her glittering eye. "Well, of all!"

"Is it so surprising?"

The lady gave her boat to the waves again. "Ann Apperthwaite thinks about him still!" she said, with something like vindictiveness. "I've always suspected it. She thought you were new to the place and didn't know anything about it all, or anybody to mention it to. That's it!"

"I'm still new to the place," I urged, "and still don't know anything about it all."

"They used to be engaged," was her succinct and emphatic answer.

I found it but too illuminating. "Oh, oh!" I cried. "I WAS an innocent, wasn't I?"

"I'm glad she DOES think of him," said my cousin. "It serves her right. I only hope HE won't find it out, because he's a poor, faithful creature; he'd jump at the chance to take her back—and she doesn't deserve him."

"How long has it been," I asked, "since they used to be engaged?"

"Oh, a good while—five or six years ago, I think—maybe more; time skips along. Ann Apperthwaite's no chicken, you know." (Such was the lady's expression.) "They got engaged just after she came home from college, and of all the idiotically romantic girls—"

"But she's a teacher," I interrupted, "of mathematics."

"Yes." She nodded wisely. "I always thought that explained it: the romance is a reaction from the algebra. I never knew a person connected with mathematics or astronomy or statistics, or any of those exact things, who didn't have a crazy streak in 'em SOMEwhere. They've got to blow off steam and be foolish to make up for putting in so much of their time at hard sense. But don't you think that I dislike Ann Apperthwaite. She's always been one of my best friends; that's why I feel at liberty to abuse her—and I always will abuse her when I think how she treated poor David Beasley."

"How did she treat him?"

"Threw him over out of a clear sky one night, that's all. Just sent him home and broke his heart; that is, it would have been broken if he'd had any kind of disposition except the one the Lord blessed him with—just all optimism and cheerfulness and make-the-best-of-it-ness! He's never cared for anybody else, and I guess he never will."

"What did she do it for?"

"NOTHING!" My cousin shot the indignant word from her lips. "Nothing in the wide WORLD!"

"But there must have been—"

"Listen to me," she interrupted, "and tell me if you ever heard anything queerer in your life. They'd been engaged—Heaven knows how long—over two years; probably nearer three—and always she kept putting it off; wouldn't begin to get ready, wouldn't set a day for the wedding. Then Mr. Apperthwaite died, and left her and her mother stranded high and dry with nothing to live on. David had everything in the world to give her—and STILL she wouldn't! And then, one day, she came up here and told me she'd broken it off. Said she couldn't stand it to be engaged to David Beasley another minute!"

"But why?"

"Because"—my cousin's tone was shrill with her despair of expressing the satire she would have put into it—"because, she said he was a man of no imagination!"

"She still says so," I remarked, thoughtfully.

"Then it's time she got a little imagination herself!" snapped my companion. "David Beasley's the quietest man God has made, but everybody knows what he IS! There are some rare people in this world that aren't all TALK; there are some still rarer ones that scarcely ever talk at all —and David Beasley's one of them. I don't know whether it's because he can't talk, or if he can and hates to; I only know he doesn't. And I'm glad of it, and thank the Lord he's put a few like that into this talky world! David Beasley's smile is better than acres of other people's talk. My Providence! Wouldn't anybody, just to look at him, know that he does better than talk? He THINKS! The trouble with Ann Apperthwaite was that she was too young to see it. She was so full of novels and poetry and dreaminess and highfalutin nonsense she couldn't see ANYTHING as it really was. She'd study her mirror, and see such a heroine of romance there that she just couldn't bear to have a fiance who hadn't any chance of turning out to be the crown-prince of Kenosha in disguise! At the very least, to suit HER he'd have had to wear a 'well-trimmed Vandyke' and coo sonnets in the gloaming, or read On a Balcony to her by a red lamp.

"Poor David! Outside of his law-books, I don't believe he's ever read anything but Robinson Crusoe and the Bible and Mark Twain. Oh, you should have heard her talk about it!—'I couldn't bear it another day,' she said, 'I couldn't STAND it! In all the time I've known him I don't believe he's ever asked me a single question—except when he asked if I'd marry him. He never says ANYTHING—never speaks at ALL!' she said. 'You don't know a blessing when you see it,' I told her. 'Blessing!' she said. 'There's nothing IN the man! He has no DEPTHS! He hasn't any more imagination than the chair he sits and sits and sits in! Half the time he answers what I say to him by nodding and saying 'um-hum,' with that same old foolish, contented smile of his. I'd have gone MAD if it had lasted any longer!' I asked her if she thought married life consisted very largely of conversations between husband and wife; and she answered that even married life ought to have some POETRY in it. 'Some romance,' she said, 'some soul! And he just comes and sits,' she said, 'and sits and sits and sits and sits! And I can't bear it any longer, and I've told him so.'"

"Poor Mr. Beasley," I said.

"*I* think, 'Poor Ann Apperthwaite!'" retorted my cousin. "I'd like to know if there's anything NICER than just to sit and sit and sit and sit with as lovely a man as that—a man who understands things, and thinks and listens and smiles—instead of everlastingly talking!"

"As it happens," I remarked, "I've heard Mr. Beasley talk."

"Why, of course he talks," she returned, "when there's any real use in it. And he talks to children; he's THAT kind of man."

"I meant a particular instance," I began; meaning to see if she could give me any clew to Bill Hammersley and Simpledoria, but at that moment the gate clicked under the hand of another caller. My cousin rose to greet him; and presently I took my leave without having been able to get back upon the subject of Beasley.

Thus, once more baffled, I returned to Mrs. Apperthwaite's—and within the hour came into full possession of the very heart of that dark and subtle mystery which overhung the house next door and so perplexed my soul.

IV

Finding that I had still some leisure before me, I got a book from my room and repaired to the bench in the garden. But I did not read; I had but opened the book when my attention was arrested by sounds from the other side of the high fence—low and tremulous croonings of distinctly African derivation:

"Ah met mah sistuh in a-mawnin',
She 'uz a-waggin' up de hill SO slow!
'Sistuh, you mus' git a rastle in doo time,
B'fo de hevumly do's cloze—iz!'"

It was the voice of an aged negro; and the simultaneous slight creaking of a small hub and axle seemed to indicate that he was pushing or pulling a child's wagon or perambulator up and down the walk from the kitchen door to the stable. Whiles, he proffered soothing music: over and over he repeated the chant, though with variations; encountering in turn his brother, his daughter, each of his parents, his uncle, his cousin, and his second-cousin, one after the other ascending the same slope with the same perilous leisure.

"Lay still, honey." He interrupted his injunctions to the second-cousin. "Des keep on a-nappin' an' a-breavin' de f'esh air. Dass wha's go' mek you good an' well agin."

Then there spoke the strangest voice that ever fell upon my ear; it was not like a child's, neither was it like a very old person's voice; it might have been a grasshopper's, it was so thin and little, and made of such tiny wavers and quavers and creakings.

"I—want—" said this elfin voice, "I—want—Bill—Hammersley!"

The shabby phaeton which had passed my cousin's house was drawing up to the curb near Beasley's gate. Evidently the old negro saw it.

"Hi dar!" he exclaimed. "Look at dat! Hain' Bill a comin' yonnah des edzacly on de dot an' to de vey spot an' instink when you 'quiah fo' 'im, honey? Dar come Mist' Dave, right on de minute, an' you kin bet yo' las hunnud dollahs he got dat Bill Hammersley wif 'im! Come along, honey-chile! Ah's go' to pull you 'roun in de side yod fo' to meet 'em."

The small wagon creaked away, the chant resuming as it went.

Mr. Dowden jumped out of the phaeton with a wave of his hand to the driver, Beasley himself, who clucked to the horse and drove through his open carriage-gates and down the drive on the other side of the house, where he was lost to my view.

Dowden, entering our own gate, nodded in a friendly fashion to me, and I advanced to meet him.

"Some day I want to take you over next door," he said, cordially, as I came up. "You ought to know Beasley, especially as I hear you're doing some political reporting. Dave Beasley's going to be the next governor of this state, you know." He laughed, offered me a cigar, and we sat down together on the front steps.

"From all I hear," I rejoined, "YOU ought to know who'll get it." (It was said in town that Dowden would "come pretty near having the nomination in his pocket.")

"I expect you thought I shifted the subject pretty briskly the other day?" He glanced at me quizzically from under the brim of his black felt hat. "I meant to tell you about that, but the opportunity didn't occur. You see—"

"I understand," I interrupted. "I've heard the story. You thought it might be embarrassing to Miss Apperthwaite."

"I expect I was pretty clumsy about it," said Dowden, cheerfully. "Well, well—" he flicked his cigar with a smothered ejaculation that was half a sigh and half a laugh; "it's a mighty strange case. Here they keep on living next door to each other, year after year, each going on alone when they might just as well—" He left the sentence unfinished, save for a vocal click of compassion. "They bow when they happen to meet, but they haven't exchanged a word since the night she sent him away, long ago." He shook his head, then his countenance cleared and he chuckled. "Well, sir, Dave's got something at home to keep him busy enough, these days, I expect!"

"Do you mind telling me?" I inquired. "Is its name 'Simpledoria'?"

Mr. Dowden threw back his head and laughed loudly. "Lord, no! What on earth made you think that?"

I told him. It was my second success with this narrative; however, there was a difference: my former auditor listened with flushed and breathless excitement, whereas the present one laughed consumedly throughout. Especially he laughed with a great laughter at the picture of Beasley's coming down at four in the morning to open the door for nothing on sea or land or in the waters under the earth. I gave account, also, of the miraculous jumping contest (though I did not mention Miss Apperthwaite's having been with me), and of the elfin voice I had just now overheard demanding "Bill Hammersley."

"So I expect you must have decided," he chuckled, when I concluded, "that David Beasley has gone just plain, plum insane."

"Not a bit of it. Nobody could look at him and not know better than that."

"You're right THERE!" said Dowden, heartily. "And now I'll tell you all there is TO it. You see, Dave grew up with a cousin of his named Hamilton Swift; they were boys together; went to the same school, and then to college. I don't believe there was ever a high word spoken between them. Nobody in this life ever got a quarrel out of Dave Beasley, and Hamilton Swift was a mighty good sort of a fellow, too. He went East to live, after they got out of college, yet they always managed to get together once a year, generally about Christmas-time; you couldn't pass them on the street without hearing their laughter ringing out louder than the sleigh-bells, maybe over some old joke between them, or some fool thing they did, perhaps, when they were boys. But finally Hamilton Swift's business took him over to the other side of the water to live; and he married an English girl, an orphan without any kin. That was about seven years ago. Well, sir, this last summer he and his wife were taking a trip down in Switzerland, and they were both drowned—tipped over out of a rowboat in Lake Lucerne—and word came that Hamilton Swift's will appointed Dave guardian of the one child they had, a little boy—Hamilton Swift, Junior's his name. He was sent across the ocean in charge of a doctor, and Dave went on to New York to meet him. He brought him home here the very day before you passed the house and saw poor Dave getting up at four in the morning to let that ghost in. And a mighty funny ghost Simpledoria is!"

"I begin to understand," I said, "and to feel pretty silly, too."

"Not at all," he rejoined, heartily. "That little chap's freaks would mystify anybody, especially with Dave humoring 'em the ridiculous way he does. Hamilton Swift, Junior, is the curiousest child I ever saw—and the good Lord knows He made all children powerful mysterious! This poor little cuss has a complication of infirmities that have kept him on his back most of his life, never knowing other children, never playing, or anything; and he's got ideas and ways that I never saw the beat of! He was born sick, as I understand it—his bones and nerves and insides are all wrong, somehow—but it's supposed he gets a little better from year to year. He wears a pretty elaborate set of braces, and he's subject to attacks, too—I don't know the name for 'em—and loses what little voice he has sometimes, all but a whisper. He had one, I know, the day after Beasley brought him home, and that was probably the reason you thought Dave was carrying on all to himself about that jumping-match out in the back-yard. The boy must have been lying there in the little wagon they have for him, while Dave cut up shines with 'Bill Hammersley.' Of course, most children have make-believe friends and companions, especially if they haven't any brothers or sisters, but this lonely little feller's got HIS people worked out in his mind and materialized beyond any I ever heard of. Dave got well acquainted with 'em on the train on the way home, and they certainly are giving him a lively time. Ho, ho! Getting him up at four in the morning—"

Mr. Dowden's mirth overcame him for a moment; when he had mastered it, he continued: "Simpledoria—now where do you suppose he got that name?—well, anyway, Simpledoria is supposed to be Hamilton Swift, Junior's St. Bernard dog. Beasley had to BATHE him the other day, he told me! And Bill Hammersley is supposed to be a boy of Hamilton Swift, Junior's own age, but very big and strong; he has rosy cheeks, and he can do more in athletics than a whole college track-team. That's the reason he outjumped Dave so far, you see."

V

Miss Apperthwaite was at home the following Saturday. I found her in the library with Les Miserables on her knee when I came down from my room a little before lunch-time; and she looked up and gave me a smile that made me feel sorry for any one she had ceased to smile upon.

"I wanted to tell you," I said, with a little awkwardness but plenty of truth, "I've found out that I'm an awful fool."

"But that's something," she returned, encouragingly—"at least the beginning of wisdom."

"I mean about Mr. Beasley—the mystery I was absurd enough to find in 'Simpledoria.' I want to tell you—"

"Oh, *I* know," she said; and although she laughed with an effect of carelessness, that look which I had thought "far away" returned to her eyes as she spoke. There was a certain inscrutability about Miss Apperthwaite sometimes, it should be added, as if she did not like to be too easily read. "I've heard all about it. Mr. Beasley's been appointed trustee or something for poor Hamilton Swift's son, a pitiful little invalid boy who invents all sorts of characters. The old darky from over there told our cook about Bill Hammersley and Simpledoria. So, you see, I understand."

"I'm glad you do," I said.

A little hardness—one might even have thought it bitterness—became apparent in her expression. "And I'm glad there's SOMEbody in that house, at last, with a little imagination!"

"From everything I have heard," I returned, summoning sufficient boldness, "it would be difficult to say which has more—Mr. Beasley or the child."

Her glance fell from mine at this, but not quickly enough to conceal a sudden, half-startled look of trouble (I can think of no other way to express it) that leaped into it; and she rose, for the lunch-bell was ringing.

"I'm just finishing the death of Jean Valjean, you know, in Les Miserables," she said, as we moved to the door. "I'm always afraid I'll cry over that. I try not to, because it makes my eyes red."

And, in truth, there was a vague rumor of tears about her eyes—not as if she had shed them, but more as if she were going to—though I had not noticed it when I came in.

... That afternoon, when I reached the "Despatch" office, I was commissioned to obtain certain political information from the Honorable David Beasley, an assignment I accepted with eagerness, notwithstanding the commiseration it brought me from one or two of my fellows in the reporter's room. "You won't get anything out of HIM!" they said. And they were true prophets.

I found him looking over some documents in his office; a reflective, unlighted cigar in the corner of his mouth; his chair tilted back and his feet on a window-sill. He nodded, upon my statement of the affair that brought me, and, without shifting his position, gave me a look of slow but wholly friendly scrutiny over his shoulder, and bade me sit down. I began at once to put the questions I was told to ask him—interrogations (he seemed to believe) satisfactorily answered by slowly and ruminatively stroking the left side of his chin with two long fingers of his right hand, the while he smiled in genial contemplation of a tarred roof beyond the window. Now and then he would give me a mild and drawling word or two, not brilliantly illuminative, it may be remarked. "Well—about that—" he began once, and came immediately to a full stop.

"Yes?" I said, hopefully, my pencil poised.

"About that—I guess—"

"Yes, Mr. Beasley?" I encouraged him, for he seemed to have dried up permanently.

"Well, sir—I guess—Hadn't you better see some one else about THAT?"

This with the air of a man who would be but too fluent and copious upon any subject in the world except the one particular point.

I never met anybody else who looked so pleasantly communicative and managed to say so little. In fact, he didn't say anything at all; and I guessed that this faculty was not without its value in his political career, disastrous as it had proved to his private happiness. His habit of silence, moreover, was not cultivated: you could see that "the secret of it" was just that he was BORN quiet.

My note-book remained noteless, and finally, at some odd evasion of his, accomplished by a monosyllable, I laughed outright—and he did, too! He joined cachinnations with me heartily, and with a twinkling quizzicalness that somehow gave me the idea that he might be thinking (rather apologetically) to himself: "Yes, sir, that old Beasley man is certainly a mighty funny critter!"

When I went away, a few moments later, and left him still intermittently chuckling, the impression remained with me that he had had some such deprecatory and surreptitious thought.

Two or three days after that, as I started down-town from Mrs. Apperthwaite's, Beasley came out of his gate, bound in the same direction. He gave me a look of gay recognition and offered his hand, saying, "WELL! Up in THIS neighborhood!" as if that were a matter of considerable astonishment.

I mentioned that I was a neighbor, and we walked on together. I don't think he spoke again, except for a "Well, sir!" or two of genial surprise at something I said, and, now and then, "You don't tell me!" which he had a most eloquent way of exclaiming; but he listened visibly to my own talk, and laughed at everything that I meant for funny.

I never knew anybody who gave one a greater responsiveness; he seemed to be WITH you every instant; and HOW he made you feel it was the true mystery of Beasley, this silent man who never talked, except (as my cousin said) to children.

It happened that I thus met him, as we were both starting down-town, and walked on with him, several days in succession; in a word, it became a habit. Then, one afternoon, as I turned to leave him at the "Despatch" office, he asked me if I wouldn't drop in at his house the next day for a cigar before we started. I did; and he asked me if I wouldn't come again the day after that. So this became a habit, too.

A fortnight elapsed before I met Hamilton Swift, Junior; for he, poor little father of dream-children, could be no spectator of track events upon the lawn, but lay in his bed up-stairs. However, he grew better at last, and my presentation took place.

We had just finished our cigars in Beasley's airy, old-fashioned "sitting-room," and were rising to go, when there came the faint creaking of small wheels from the hall. Beasley turned to me with the apologetic and monosyllabic chuckle that was distinctly his alone.

"I've got a little chap here——" he said; then went to the door. "Bob!"

The old darky appeared in the doorway pushing a little wagon like a reclining-chair on wheels, and in it sat Hamilton Swift, Junior.

My first impression of him was that he was all eyes: I couldn't look at anything else for a time, and was hardly conscious of the rest of that weazened, peaked little face and the under-sized wisp of a body with its pathetic adjuncts of metal and leather. I think they were the brightest eyes I ever saw—as keen and intelligent as a wicked old woman's, withal as trustful and cheery as the eyes of a setter pup.

"HOO-ray!"

Thus the Honorable Mr. Beasley, waving a handkerchief thrice around his head and thrice cheering.

And the child, in that cricket's voice of his, replied:

"Br-r-ra-vo!"

This was the form of salutation familiarly in use between them. Beasley followed it by inquiring, "Who's with us to-day?"

"I'm MISTER Swift," chirped the little fellow. "MIS-TER Swift, if you please, Cousin David Beasley."

Beasley executed a formal bow. "There is a gentleman here who'd like to meet you." And he presented me with some grave phrases commendatory of my general character, addressing the child as "Mister Swift"; whereupon Mister Swift gave me a ghostly little hand and professed himself glad to meet me.

"And besides me," he added, to Beasley, "there's Bill Hammersley and Mr. Corley Linbridge."

A faint perplexity manifested itself upon Beasley's face at this, a shadow which cleared at once when I asked if I might not be permitted to meet these personages, remarking that I had heard from Dowden of Bill Hammersley, though until now a stranger to the fame of Mr. Corley Linbridge.

Beasley performed the ceremony with intentional elegance, while the boy's great eyes swept glowingly from his cousin's face to mine and back again. I bowed and shook hands with the air, once to my left and once to my right. "And Simpledoria!" cried Mister Swift. "You'll enjoy Simpledoria."

"Above all things," I said. "Can he shake hands? Some dogs can."

"Watch him!"

Mister Swift lifted a commanding finger. "Simpledoria, shake hands!"

I knelt beside the wagon and shook an imaginary big paw. At this Mister Swift again shook hands with me and allowed me to perceive, in his luminous regard, a solemn commendation and approval.

In this wise was my initiation into the beautiful old house and the cordiality of its inmates completed; and I became a familiar of David

Beasley and his ward, with the privilege to go and come as I pleased; there was always gay and friendly welcome. I always came for the cigar after lunch, sometimes for lunch itself; sometimes I dined there instead of downtown; and now and then when it happened that an errand or assignment took me that way in the afternoon, I would run in and "visit" awhile with Hamilton Swift, Junior, and his circle of friends.

There were days, of course, when his attacks were upon him, and only Beasley and the doctor and old Bob saw him; I do not know what the boy's mental condition was at such times; but when he was better, and could be wheeled about the house and again receive callers, he displayed an almost dismaying activity of mind—it was active enough, certainly, to keep far ahead of my own. And he was masterful: still, Beasley and Dowden and I were never directly chidden for insubordination, though made to wince painfully by the look of troubled surprise that met us when we were not quick enough to catch his meaning.

The order of the day with him always began with the "HOO-ray" and "BR-R-RA-vo" of greeting; after which we were to inquire, "Who's with us to-day?" Whereupon he would make known the character in which he elected to be received for the occasion. If he announced himself as "Mister Swift," everything was to be very grown-up and decorous indeed. Formalities and distances were observed; and Mr. Corley Linbridge (an elderly personage of great dignity and distinction as a mountain-climber) was much oftener included in the conversation than Bill Hammersley. If, however, he declared himself to be "Hamilton Swift, Junior," which was his happiest mood, Bill Hammersley and Simpledoria were in the ascendant, and there were games and contests. (Dowden, Beasley, and I all slid down the banisters on one of the Hamilton Swift, Junior, days, at which really picturesque spectacle the boy almost cried with laughter—and old Bob and his wife, who came running from the kitchen, DID cry.) He had a third appellation for himself—"Just little Hamilton"; but this was only when the creaky voice could hardly chirp at all and the weazened face was drawn to one side with suffering. When he told us he was "Just little Hamilton" we were very quiet.

Once, for ten days, his Invisibles all went away on a visit: Hamilton Swift, Junior, had become interested in bears. While this lasted, all of Beasley's trousers were, as Dowden said, "a sight." For that matter, Dowden himself was quite hoarse in court from growling so much. The bears were dismissed abruptly: Bill Hammersley and Mr. Corley Linbridge and Simpledoria came trooping back, and with them they brought that wonderful family, the Hunchbergs.

Beasley had just opened the front door, returning at noon from his office, when Hamilton Swift, Junior's voice came piping from the library, where he was reclining in his wagon by the window.

"Cousin David Beasley! Cousin David, come a-running!" he cried. "Come a-running! The Hunchbergs are here!"

Of course Cousin David Beasley came a-running, and was immediately introduced to the whole Hunchberg family, a ceremony which old Bob, who was with the boy, had previously undergone with courtly grace.

"They like Bob," explained Hamilton. "Don't you, Mr. Hunchberg? Yes, he says they do extremely!" (He used such words as "extremely" often; indeed, as Dowden said, he talked "like a child in a book," which was due, I dare say, to his English mother.) "And I'm sure," the boy went on, "that all the family will admire Cousin David. Yes, Mr. Hunchberg says, he thinks they will."

And then (as Bob told me) he went almost out of his head with joy when Beasley offered Mr. Hunchberg a cigar and struck a match for him to light it.

"But WHAR," exclaimed the old darky, "whar in de name o' de good Gawd do de chile git dem NAMES? Hit lak to SKEER me!"

That was a subject often debated between Dowden and me: there was nothing in Wainwright that could have suggested them, and it did not seem probable he could have remembered them from over the water. In my opinion they were the inventions of that busy and lonely little brain.

I met the Hunchberg family, myself, the day after their arrival, and Beasley, by that time, had become so well acquainted with them that he could remember all their names, and helped in the introductions. There was Mr. Hunchberg—evidently the child's favorite, for he was described as the possessor of every engaging virtue—and there was that lively matron, Mrs. Hunchberg; there were the Hunchberg young gentlemen, Tom, Noble, and Grandee; and the young ladies, Miss Queen, Miss Marble, and Miss Molanna—all exceedingly gay and pretty. There was also Colonel Hunchberg, an uncle; finally there was Aunt Cooley Hunchberg, a somewhat decrepit but very amiable old lady. Mr. Corley Linbridge happened to be calling at the same time; and, as it appeared to be Beasley's duty to keep the conversation going and constantly to include all of the party in its general flow, it struck me that he had truly (as Dowden said) "enough to keep him busy."

The Hunchbergs had lately moved to Wainwright from Constantinople, I learned; they had decided not to live in town, however, having purchased a fine farm out in the country, and, on account of the distance, were able to call at Beasley's only about eight times a day, and seldom more than twice in the evening. Whenever a mystic telephone announced that they were on the way, the child would have himself wheeled to a window; and when they came in sight he would cry out in wild delight, while Beasley hastened to open the front door and admit them.

They were so real to the child, and Beasley treated them with such consistent seriousness, that between the two of them I sometimes began to feel that there actually were such people, and to have moments of half-surprise that I couldn't see them; particularly as each of the Hunchberg's developed a character entirely his own to the last peculiarity, such as the aged Aunt Cooley Hunchberg's deafness, on which account Beasley never once forgot to raise his voice when he addressed her. Indeed, the details of actuality in all this appeared to bring as great a delight to the man as to the child. Certainly he built them up with infinite care. On one occasion when Mr. Hunchberg and I happened to be calling, Hamilton remarked with surprise that Simpledoria had come into the room without licking his hand as he usually did, and had crept under the table. Mr. Hunchberg volunteered the information (through Beasley) that upon his approach to the house he had seen Simpledoria chasing a cat. It was then debated whether chastisement was in order, but finally decided that Simpledoria's surreptitious manner of entrance and his hiding under the table were sufficient indication that he well understood his baseness, and would never let it happen again. And so, Beasley having coaxed him out from under the table, the offender "sat up," begged, and was forgiven. I could almost feel the splendid shaggy head under my hand when, in turn, I patted Simpledoria to show that the reconciliation unanimous.

VI

Autumn trailed the last leaves behind her flying brown robes one night; we woke to a skurry of snow next morning; and it was winter. Down-town, along the sidewalks, the merchants set lines of poles, covered them with evergreen, and ran streamers of green overhead to encourage the festal shopping. Salvation Army Santa Clauses stamped their feet and rang bells on the corners, and pink-faced children fixed their noses immovably to display-windows. For them, the season of seasons, the time of times, was at hand.

To a certain new reporter on the "Despatch" the stir and gayety of the streets meant little more than that the days had come when it was night in the afternoon, and that he was given fewer political assignments. This was annoying, because Beasley's candidacy for the governorship had given me a personal interest in the political situation. The nominating convention of his party would meet in the spring; the nomination was certain to carry the election also, and thus far Beasley showed more strength than any other man in the field. "Things are looking his way," said Dowden. "He's always worked hard for the party; not on the stump, of course," he laughed; "but the boys understand there are more important things than speech-making. His record in Congress gave him the confidence of everybody in the state, and, besides that, people always trust a quiet man. I tell you if nothing happens he'll get it."

"I'm FER Beasley," another politician explained, in an interview, "because he's Dave Beasley! Yes, sir, I'm FER him. You know the boys say if a man is only FOR you, in this state, there isn't much in it and he may go back on it; but if he's FER you, he means it. Well, I'm FER Beasley!"

There were other candidates, of course; none of them formidable; but I was surprised to learn of the existence of a small but energetic faction opposing our friend in Wainwright, his own town. ("What are you surprised about?" inquired Dowden. "Don't you know what our folks are like, YET? If St. Paul lived in Wainwright, do you suppose he could run for constable without some of his near neighbors getting out to try and down him?")

The head and front (and backbone, too) of the opposition to Beasley was a close-fisted, hard-knuckled, risen-from-the-soil sort of man, one named Simeon Peck. He possessed no inconsiderable influence, I heard; was a hard worker, and vigorously seconded by an energetic lieutenant, a young man named Grist. These, and others they had been able to draw to their faction, were bitterly and eagerly opposed to Beasley's nomination, and worked without ceasing to prevent it.

I quote the invaluable Mr. Dowden again: "Grist's against us because he had a quarrel with a clerk in Beasley's office, and wanted Beasley to discharge him, and Beasley wouldn't; Sim Peck's against us out of just plain wrong-headedness, and because he never was for ANYTHING nor FER anybody in his life. I had a talk with the old mutton-head the other day; he said our candidate ought to be a farmer, a 'man of the common people,' and when I asked him where he'd find anybody more a 'man of the common people' than Beasley, he said Beasley was 'too much of a society man' to suit him! The idea of Dave as a 'society man' was too much for me, and I laughed in Sim Peck's face, but that didn't stop Sim Peck! 'Jest look at the style he lives in,' he yelped. 'Ain't he fairly LAPPED in luxury? Look at that big house he lives in! Look at the way he goes around in that phaeton of his —and a nigger to drive him half the time!' I had to holler again, and, of course, that made Sim twice as mad as he started out to be; and he went off swearing he'd show ME, before the campaign was over. The only trouble he and Grist and that crowd could give us would be by finding out something against Dave, and they can't do that because there isn't anything to find out."

I shared his confidence on this latter score, but was somewhat less sanguine on some others. There were only two newspapers of any political influence in Wainwright, the "Despatch" and the "Journal," both operated in the interest of Beasley's party, and neither had "come out" for him. The gossip I heard about our office led me to think that each was waiting to see what headway Sim Peck and his faction would make; the "Journal" especially, I knew, had some inclination to coquette with Peck, Grist, and Company. Altogether, their faction was not entirely to be despised.

Thus, my thoughts were a great deal more occupied with Beasley's chances than with the holiday spirit that now, with furs and bells and wreathing mists of snow, breathed good cheer over the town. So little, indeed, had this spirit touched me that, one evening when one of my colleagues, standing before the grate-fire in the reporters' room, yawned and said he'd be glad when to-morrow was over, I asked him what was the particular trouble with to-morrow.

"Christmas," he explained, languidly. "Always so tedious. Like Sunday."

"It makes me homesick," said another, a melancholy little man who was forever bragging of his native Duluth.

"Christmas," I repeated—"to-morrow!"

It was Christmas Eve, and I had not known it! I leaned back in my chair in sudden loneliness, what pictures coming before me of long-ago Christmas Eves at home!—old Christmas Eves when there was a Tree....

My name was called; the night City Editor had an assignment for me. "Go up to Sim Peck's, on Madison Street," he said. "He thinks he's got something on David Beasley, but won't say any more over the telephone. See what there is in it."

I picked up my hat and coat, and left the office at a speed which must have given my superior the highest conception of my journalistic zeal. At a telephone station on the next corner I called up Mrs. Apperthwaite's house and asked for Dowden.

"What are you doing?" I demanded, when his voice had responded.

"Playing bridge," he answered.

"Are you going out anywhere?"

"No. What's the trouble?"

"I'll tell you later. I may want to see you before I go back to the office."

"All right. I'll be here all evening."

I hung up the receiver and made off on my errand.

Down-town the streets were crowded with the package-laden people, bending heads and shoulders to the bitter wind, which swept a blinding, sleet-like snow horizontally against them. At corners it struck so tumultuous a blow upon the chest of the pedestrians that for a moment it would halt them, and you could hear them gasping half-smothered "AHS" like bathers in a heavy surf. Yet there was a gayety in this eager gale; the crowds pressed anxiously, yet happily, up and down the street in their generous search for things to give away. It was not the rich who struggled through the storm to-night; these were people who carried their own bundles home. You saw them: toilers and savers, tired mothers and fathers, worn with the grinding thrift of all the year, but now for this one night careless of how hard-saved the money, reckless of everything but the joy of giving it to bring the children joy on the one great to-morrow. So they bent their heads to the freezing wind, their arms laden with daring bundles and their hearts uplifted with the tremulous happiness of giving more than they could afford. Meanwhile, Mr. Simeon Peck, honest man, had chosen this season to work harm if he might to the gentlest of his fellow-men.

I found Mr. Peck waiting for me at his house. There were four other men with him, one of whom I recognized as Grist, a squat young man with slippery-looking black hair and a lambrequin mustache. They were donning their coats and hats in the hall when I arrived.

"From the 'Despatch,' hay?" Mr. Peck gave me greeting, as he wound a knit comforter about his neck. "That's good. We'd most give you up. This here's Mr. Grist, and Mr. Henry P. Cullop, and Mr. Gus Schulmeyer—three men that feel the same way about Dave Beasley that I do. That other young feller," he waved a mittened hand to the fourth man—"he's from the 'Journal.' Likely you're acquainted."

The young man from the 'Journal' was unknown to me; moreover, I was far from overjoyed at his presence.

"I've got you newspaper men here," continued Mr. Peck, "because I'm goin' to show you somep'n' about Dave Beasley that'll open a good many folk's eyes when it's in print."

"Well, what is it?" I asked, rather sharply.

"Jest hold your horses a little bit," he retorted. "Grist and me knows, and so do Mr. Cullop and Mr. Schulmeyer. And I'm goin' to take them and you two reporters to LOOK at it. All ready? Then come on."

He threw open the door, stooped to the gust that took him by the throat, and led the way out into the storm.

"What IS he up to?" I gasped to the "Journal" man as we followed in a straggling line.

"I don't know any more than you do," he returned. "He thinks he's got something that'll queer Beasley. Peck's an old fool, but it's just possible he's got hold of something. Nearly everybody has ONE thing, at least, that they don't want found out. It may be a good story. Lord, what a night!"

I pushed ahead to the leader's side. "See here, Mr. Peck—" I began, but he cut me off.

"You listen to ME, young man! I'm givin' you some news for your paper, and I'm gittin' at it my own way, but I'll git AT it, don't you worry! I'm goin' to let some folks around here know what kind of a feller Dave Beasley really is; yes, and I'm goin' to show George Dowden he can't laugh at ME!"

"You're going to show Mr. Dowden?" I said. "You mean you're going to take him on this expedition, too?"

"TAKE him!" Mr. Peck emitted an acrid bark of laughter. "I guess HE'S at Beasley's, all right."

"No, he isn't; he's at home—at Mrs. Apperthwaite's—playing cards."

"What!"

"I happen to know that he'll be there all evening."

Mr. Peck smote his palms together. "Grist!" he called, over his shoulder, and his colleague struggled forward. "Listen to this: even Dowden ain't at Beasley's. Ain't the Lord workin' fer us to-night!"

"Why don't you take Dowden with you," I urged, "if there's anything you want to show him?"

"By George, I WILL!" shouted Peck. "I've got him where the hair's short NOW!"

"That's right," said Grist.

"Gentlemen"—Peck turned to the others—"when we git to Mrs. Apperthwaite's, jest stop outside along the fence a minute. I recken we'll pick up a recruit."

Shivering, we took up our way again in single file, stumbling through drifts that had deepened incredibly within the hour. The wind was straight against us, and so stingingly sharp and so laden with the driving snow that when we reached Mrs. Apperthwaite's gate (which we approached from the north, not passing Beasley's) my eyes were so full of smarting tears I could see only blurred planes of light dancing vaguely in the darkness, instead of brightly lit windows.

"Now," said Peck, panting and turning his back to the wind; "the rest of you gentlemen wait out here. You two newspaper men, you come with me."

He opened the gate and went in, the "Journal" reporter and I following —all three of us wiping our half-blinded eyes. When we reached the shelter of the front porch, I took the key from my pocket and opened the door.

"I live here," I explained to Mr. Peck.

"All right," he said. "Jest step in and tell George Dowden that Sim Peck's out here and wants to see him at the door a minute. Be quick."

I went into the library, and there sat Dowden contemplatively playing bridge with two of the elderly ladies and Miss Apperthwaite. The last-mentioned person quite took my breath away.

In honor of the Christmas Eve (I supposed) she wore an evening dress of black lace, and the only word for what she looked has suffered such misuse that one hesitates over it: yet that is what she was—regal—and no less! There was a sort of splendor about her. It detracted nothing from this that her expression was a little sad: something not uncommon with her lately; a certain melancholy, faint but detectable, like breath on a mirror. I had attributed it to Jean Valjean, though perhaps to-night it might have been due merely to bridge.

"What is it?" asked Dowden, when, after an apology for disturbing the game, I had drawn him out in the hall.

I motioned toward the front door. "Simeon Peck. He thinks he's got something on Mr. Beasley. He's waiting to see you."

Dowden uttered a sharp, half-coherent exclamation and stepped quickly to the door. "Peck!" he said, as he jerked it open.

"Oh, I'm here!" declared that gentleman, stepping into view. "I've come around to let you know that you couldn't laugh like a horse at ME no more, George Dowden! So YOU weren't invited, either."

"Invited?" said Dowden, "Where?"

"Over to the BALL your friend is givin'."

"What friend?"

"Dave Beasley. So you ain't quite good enough to dance with his high-society friends!"

"What are you talking about?" Dowden demanded, impatiently.

"I reckon you won't be quite so strong fer Beasley," responded Peck, with a vindictive little giggle, "when you find he can use you in his BUSINESS, but when it comes to ENTERTAININ'—oh no, you ain't quite the boy!"

"I'd appreciate your explaining," said Dowden. "It's kind of cold standing here."

Peck laughed shrilly. "Then I reckon you better git your hat and coat and come along. Can't do US no harm, and might be an eye-opener fer YOU. Grist and Gus Schulmeyer and Hank Cullop's waitin' out yonder at the gate. We be'n havin' kind of a consultation at my house over somep'n' Grist seen at Beasley's a little earlier in the evening."

"What did Grist see?"

"HACKS! Hacks drivin' up to Beasley's house—a whole lot of 'em. Grist was down the street a piece, and it was pretty dark, but he could see the lamps and hear the doors slam as the people got out. Besides, the whole place is lit up from cellar to attic. Grist come on to my house and told me about it, and I begun usin' the telephone; called up all the men that COUNT in the party—found most of 'em at home, too. I ast 'em if they was invited to this ball to-night; and not a one of 'em was. THEY'RE only in politics; they ain't high SOCIETY enough to be ast to Mr. Beasley's dancin'-parties! But I WOULD 'a' thougnt he'd let YOU in—ANYWAYS fer the second table!" Mr. Peck shrilled out his acrid and exultant laugh again. "I got these fellers from the newspapers, and all I want is to git this here ball in print to-morrow, and see what the boys that do the work at the primaries have to say about it—and what their WIVES'll say about the man that's too high-toned to have 'em in his house. I'll bet Beasley thought he was goin' to keep these doin's quiet; afraid the farmers might not believe he's jest the plain man he sets up to be—afraid that folks like you that ain't invited might turn against him. I'LL fool him! We're goin' to see what there is to see, and I'm goin' to have these boys from the newspapers write a full account of it. If you want to come along, I expect it'll do you a power o' good."

"I'll go," said Dowden, quickly. He got his coat and hat from a table in the hall, and we rejoined the huddled and shivering group at the gate.

"Got my recruit, gents!" shrilled Peck, slapping Dowden boisterously on the shoulders. "I reckon he'll git a change of heart to-night!"

And now, sheltering my eyes from the stinging wind, I saw what I had been too blind to see as we approached Mrs. Apperthwaite's. Beasley's house WAS illuminated; every window, up stairs and down, was aglow with rosy light. That was luminously evident, although the shades were lowered.

"Look at that!" Peck turned to Dowden, giggling triumphantly. "Wha'd I tell you! How do you feel about it NOW?"

"But where are the hacks?" asked Dowden, gravely.

"Folks all come," answered Mr. Peck, with complete assurance. "Won't be no more hacks till they begin to go home."

We plunged ahead as far as the corner of Beasley's fence, where Peck stopped us again, and we drew together, slapping our hands and stamping our feet. Peck was delighted—a thoroughly happy man; his sour giggle of exultation had become continuous, and the same jovial break was audible in Grist's voice as he said to the "Journal" reporter and me:

"Go ahead, boys. Git your story. We'll wait here fer you."

The "Journal" reporter started toward the gate; he had gone, perhaps, twenty feet when Simeon Peck whistled in sharp warning. The reporter stopped short in his tracks.

Beasley's front door was thrown open, and there stood Beasley himself in evening dress, bowing and smiling, but not at us, for he did not see us. The bright hall behind him was beautiful with evergreen streamers and wreaths, and great flowering plants in jars. A strain of dance-music wandered out to us as the door opened, but there was nobody except David Beasley in sight, which certainly seemed peculiar—for a ball!

"Rest of 'em inside, dancin'," explained Mr. Peck, crouching behind the picket-fence. "I'll bet the house is more'n half full o' low-necked wimmin!"

"Sh!" said Grist. "Listen."

Beasley had begun to speak, and his voice, loud and clear, sounded over the wind. "Come right in, Colonel!" he said. "I'd have sent a carriage for you if you hadn't telephoned me this afternoon that your rheumatism was so bad you didn't expect to be able to come. I'm glad you're well again. Yes, they're all here, and the ladies are getting up a quadrille in the sitting-room."

(It was at this moment that I received upon the calf of the right leg a kick, the ecstatic violence of which led me to attribute it to Mr. Dowden.)

"Gentlemen's dressing-room up-stairs to the right, Colonel," called Beasley, as he closed the door.

There was a pause of awed silence among us.

(I improved it by returning the kick to Mr. Dowden. He made no acknowledgment of its reception other than to sink his chin a little deeper into the collar of his ulster.)

"By the Almighty!" said Simeon Peck, hoarsely. "Who—WHAT was Dave Beasley talkin' to? There wasn't nobody THERE!"

"Git out," Grist bade him; but his tone was perturbed. "He seen that reporter. He was givin' us the laugh."

"He's crazy!" exclaimed Peck, vehemently.

Immediately all four members of his party began to talk at the same time: Mr. Schulmeyer agreeing with Grist, and Mr. Cullop holding with Peck that Beasley had surely become insane; while the "Journal" man, returning, was certain that he had not been seen. Argument became a wrangle; excitement over the remarkable scene we had witnessed, and, perhaps, a certain sharpness partially engendered by the risk of freezing, led to some bitterness. High words were flung upon the wind. Eventually, Simeon Peck got the floor to himself for a moment.

"See here, boys, there's no use gittin' mad amongs' ourselves," he vociferated. "One thing we're all agreed on: nobody here never seen no such a dam peculiar performance as WE jest seen in their whole lives before. THURfore, ball or NO ball, there's somep'n' mighty wrong about this business. Ain't that so?"

They said it was.

"Well, then, there's only one thing to do—let's find out what it is."

"You bet we will."

"I wouldn't send no one in there alone," Peck went on, excitedly, "with a crazy man. Besides, I want to see what's goin' on, myself."—"So do we!" This was unanimous.

"Then let's see if there ain't some way to do it. Perhaps he ain't pulled all the shades down on the other side the house. Lots o' people fergit to do that."

There was but one mind in the party regarding this proposal. The next minute saw us all cautiously sneaking into the side yard, a ragged line of bent and flapping figures, black against the snow.

Simeon Peck's expectations were fulfilled—more than fulfilled. Not only were all the shades of the big, three-faced bay-window of the "sitting-room" lifted, but (evidently on account of the too great generosity of a huge log-fire that blazed in the old—fashioned chimney-place) one of the windows was half-raised as well. Here, in the shadow just beyond the rosy oblongs of light that fell upon the snow, we gathered and looked freely within.

Part of the room was clear to our view, though about half of it was shut off from us by the very king of all Christmas-trees, glittering with dozens and dozens of candles, sumptuous in silver, sparkling in gold, and laden with Heaven alone knows how many and what delectable enticements. Opposite the Tree, his back against the wall, sat old Bob, clad in a dress of state, part of which consisted of a swallow-tail coat (with an overgrown chrysanthemum in the buttonhole), a red necktie, and a pink-and-silver liberty cap of tissue-paper. He was scraping a fiddle "like old times come again," and the tune he played was, "Oh, my Liza, po' gal!" My feet shuffled to it in the snow.

No one except old Bob was to be seen in the room, but we watched him and listened breathlessly. When he finished "Liza," he laid the fiddle across his knee, wiped his face with a new and brilliant blue silk handkerchief, and said:

"Now come de big speech."

The Honorable David Beasley, carrying a small mahogany table, stepped out from beyond the Christmas-tree, advanced to the centre of the room; set the table down; disappeared for a moment and returned with a white water-pitcher and a glass. He placed these upon the table, bowed gracefully several times, then spoke:

"Ladies and gentleman—" There he paused.

"Well," said Mr. Simeon Peck, slowly, "don't this beat hell!"

"Look out!" The "Journal" reporter twitched his sleeve. "Ladies present."

"Where?" said I.

He leaned nearer me and spoke in a low tone. "Just behind us. She followed us over from your boarding-house. She's been standing around near us all along. I supposed she was Dowden's daughter, probably."

"He hasn't any daughter," I said, and stepped back to the hooded figure I had been too absorbed in our quest to notice.

It was Miss Apperthwaite.

She had thrown a loose cloak over her head and shoulders; but enveloped in it as she was, and crested and epauletted with white, I knew her at once. There was no mistaking her, even in a blizzard.

She caught my hand with a strong, quick pressure, and, bending her head to mine, said, close to my ear:

"I heard everything that man said in our hallway. You left the library door open when you called Mr. Dowden out."

"So," I returned, maliciously, "you—you couldn't HELP following!"

She released my hand—gently, to my surprise.

"Hush," she whispered. "He's saying something."

"Ladies and gentlemen," said Beasley again—and stopped again.

Dowden's voice sounded hysterically in my right ear. (Miss Apperthwaite had whispered in my left.) "The only speech he's ever made in his life—and he's stuck!"

But Beasley wasn't: he was only deliberating.

"Ladies and gentlemen," he began—"Mr. and Mrs. Hunchberg, Colonel Hunchberg and Aunt Cooley Hunchberg, Miss Molanna, Miss Queen, and Miss Marble Hunchberg, Mr. Noble, Mr. Tom, and Mr. Grandee Hunchberg, Mr. Corley Linbridge, and Master Hammersley:—You see before you to-night, my person, merely the representative of your real host. MISTER Swift. Mister Swift has expressed a wish that there should be a speech, and has deputed me to make it. He requests that the subject he has assigned me should be treated in as dignified a manner as is possible—considering the orator. Ladies and gentlemen"—he took a sip of water—"I will now address you upon the following subject: 'Why we Call Christmas-time the Best Time.'

"Christmas-time is the best time because it is the kindest time. Nobody ever felt very happy without feeling very kind, and nobody ever felt very kind without feeling at least a LITTLE happy. So, of course, either way about, the happiest time is the kindest time—that's THIS time. The most beautiful things our eyes can see are the stars; and for that reason, and in remembrance of One star, we set candles on the Tree to be stars in the house. So we make Christmas-time a time of stars indoors; and they shine warmly against the cold outdoors that is like the cold of other seasons not so kind. We set our hundred candles on the Tree and keep them bright throughout the Christmas-time, for while they shine upon us we have light to see this life, not as a battle, but as the march of a mighty Fellowship! Ladies and gentlemen, I thank you!"

He bowed to right and left, as to an audience politely applauding, and, lifting the table and its burden, withdrew; while old Bob again set his fiddle to his chin and scraped the preliminary measures of a quadrille.

Beasley was back in an instant, shouting as he came: "TAKE your pardners! Balance ALL!"

And then and there, and all by himself, he danced a quadrille, performing at one and the same time for four lively couples. Never in my life have I seen such gyrations and capers as were cut by that long-legged, loose-jointed, miraculously flying figure. He was in the wildest motion without cessation, never the fraction of an instant still; calling the figures at the top of his voice and dancing them simultaneously; his expression anxious but polite (as is the habit of other dancers); his hands extended as if to swing his partner or corner, or "opposite lady"; and his feet lifting high and flapping down in an old-fashioned step. "FIRST four, forward and back!" he shouted. "Forward and SALUTE! BALANCE to corners! SWING pardners! GR-R-RAND Right-and-Left!"

I think the combination of abandon and decorum with which he performed that "Grand Right-and-Left" was the funniest thing I have ever seen. But I didn't laugh at it.

Neither did Miss Apperthwaite.

"NOW do you believe me?" Peck was arguing, fiercely, with Mr. Schulmeyer. "Is he crazy, or ain't he?"

"He is," Grist agreed, hoarsely. "He is a stark, starin', ravin', roarin' lunatic! And the nigger's humorin' him!"

They were all staring, open-mouthed and aghast, into the lighted room.

"Do you see where it puts US?" Simeon Peck's rasping voice rose high.

"I guess I do!" said Grist. "We come out to buy a barn, and got a house and lot fer the same money. It's the greatest night's work you ever done, Sim Peck!"

"I guess it is!"

"Shake on it, Sim."

They shook hands, exalted with triumph.

"This'll do the work," giggled Peck. "It's about two-thousand per cent, better than the story we started to git. Why, Dave Beasley'll be in a padded cell in a month! It'll be all over town to-morrow, and he'll have as much chance fer governor as that nigger in there!" In his ecstasy he smote Dowden deliriously in the ribs. "What do you think of your candidate NOW?"

"Wait," said Dowden. "Who came in the hacks that Grist saw?"

This staggered Mr. Peck. He rubbed his mitten over his woollen cap as if scratching his head. "Why," he said, slowly—"who in Halifax DID come in them hacks?"

"The Hunchbergs," said I.

"Who's the Hunchbergs? Where—"

"Listen," said Dowden.

"FIRST couple, FACE out!" shouted Beasley, facing out with an invisible lady on his akimboed arm, while old Bob sawed madly at A New Coon in Town.

"SECOND couple, FALL in!" Beasley wheeled about and enacted the second couple.

"THIRD couple!" He fell in behind himself again.

"FOURTH couple, IF you please! BALANCE—ALL!—I beg your pardon, Miss Molanna, I'm afraid I stepped on your train.—SASHAY ALL!"

After the "sashay"—the noblest and most dashing bit of gymnastics displayed in the whole quadrille—he bowed profoundly to his invisible partner and came to a pause, wiping his streaming face. Old Bob dexterously swung A New Coon into the stately measures of a triumphal march.

"And now," Beasley announced, in stentorian tones, "if the ladies will be so kind as to take the gentlemen's arms, we will proceed to the dining-room and partake of a slight collation."

Thereupon came a slender piping of joy from that part of the room screened from us by the Tree.

"Oh, Cousin David Beasley, that was the BEAUTIFULLEST quadrille ever danced in the world! And, please, won't YOU take Mrs. Hunchberg out to supper?"

Then into the vision of our paralyzed and dumfounded watchers came the little wagon, pulled by the old colored woman, Bob's wife, in her best, and there, propped upon pillows, lay Hamilton Swift, Junior, his soul shining rapture out of his great eyes, a bright spot of color on each of his thin cheeks. He lifted himself on one elbow, and for an instant something seemed to be wrong with the brace under his chin.

Beasley sprang to him and adjusted it tenderly. Then he bowed elaborately toward the mantel-piece.

"Mrs. Hunchberg," he said, "may I have the honor?" And offered his arm.

"And I must have MISTER Hunchberg," chirped Hamilton. "He must walk with me."

"He tells ME," said Beasley, "he'll be mighty glad to. And there's a plate of bones for Simpledoria."

"You lead the way," cried the child; "you and Mrs. Hunchberg."

"Are we all in line?" Beasley glanced back over his shoulder. "HOO-ray! Now, let us on. Ho! there!"

"BR-R-RA-vo!" applauded Mister Swift.

And Beasley, his head thrown back and his chest out, proudly led the way, stepping nobly and in time to the exhilarating measures. Hamilton Swift, Junior, towed by the beaming old mammy, followed in his wagon, his thin little arm uplifted and his fingers curled as if they held a trusted hand.

When they reached the door, old Bob rose, turned in after them, and, still fiddling, played the procession and himself down the hall.

And so they marched away, and we were left staring into the empty room....

"My soul!" said the "Journal" reporter, gasping. "And he did all THAT —just to please a little sick kid!"

"I can't figure it out," murmured Sim Peck, piteously.

"*I* can," said the "Journal" reporter. "This story WILL be all over town to-morrow." He glanced at me, and I nodded. "It'll be all over town," he continued, "though not in any of the papers—and I don't believe it's going to hurt Dave Beasley's chances any."

Mr. Peck and his companions turned toward the street; they went silently.

The young man from the "Journal" overtook them. "Thank you for sending for me," he said, cordially. "You've given me a treat. I'm FER Beasley!"

Dowden put his hand on my shoulder. He had not observed the third figure still remaining.

"Well, sir," he remarked, shaking the snow from his coat, "they were right about one thing: it certainly was mighty low down of Dave not to invite ME—and you, too—to his Christmas party. Let him go to thunder with his old invitations, I'm going in, anyway! Come on. I'm plum froze."

There was a side door just beyond the bay-window, and Dowden went to it and rang, loud and long. It was Beasley himself who opened it.

"What in the name—" he began, as the ruddy light fell upon Dowden's face and upon me, standing a little way behind. "What ARE you two—snow-banks? What on earth are you fellows doing out here?"

"We've come to your Christmas party, you old horse-thief!" Thus Mr. Dowden.

"HOO-ray!" said Beasley.

Dowden turned to me. "Aren't you coming?"

"What are you waiting for, old fellow?" said Beasley.

I waited a moment longer, and then it happened.

She came out of the shadow and went to the foot of the steps, her cloak falling from her shoulders as she passed me. I picked it up.

She lifted her arms pleadingly, though her head was bent with what seemed to me a beautiful sort of shame. She stood there with the snow driving against her and did not speak. Beasley drew his hand slowly across his eyes—to see if they were really there, I think.

"David," she said, at last. "You've got so many lovely people in your house to-night: isn't there room for—for just one fool? It's Christmas-time!"

Printed in the USA
CPSIA information can be obtained
at www.ICGtesting.com
LVHW061316110524
780008LV00015B/1271